STREET BIKES
MOTOS DE CALLE

Connor Dayton

Traducción al español:
Eduardo Alamán

PowerKiDS press. **& Editorial Buenas Letras** IM

New York

Published in 2007 by The Rosen Publishing Group, Inc.
29 East 21st Street, New York, NY 10010

First Edition

Editor: Jennifer Way
Book Design: Erica Clendening
Layout Design: Kate Laczynski and Lissette González
Photo Researcher: Sam Cha

Photo Credits: All Photos © Shutterstock.

Cataloging Data

Dayton, Connor.
  Street bikes / Connor Dayton; traducción al español: Eduardo Alamán — 1st ed.
      p. cm. — (Motorcycles, made for speed / Motocicletas a toda velocidad)
  Includes index.
  ISBN-13: 978-1-4042-7614-7 (library binding)
  ISBN-10: 1-4042-7614-9 (library binding)
  1. Motorcycles—Juvenile literature. 2. Spanish language materials I. Title.

Manufactured in the United States of America

CONTENTS

CONTENIDO

Street bikes are the kinds of motorcycles you see every day.

Las motos de calle son el tipo de motocicletas que ves todos los días.

Some people like to ride
their bikes with others.
They might form a club
that will bike together.

A algunas personas les
gusta montar sus motos
en grupo. A veces, forman
un club de motociclistas
para pasear juntos.

People can use street bikes in their jobs. Some police officers use motorcycles instead of cars.

Muchas personas usan motos de calle en sus trabajos. Algunos policías usan motocicletas en lugar de autos.

Lots of people like to travel on their street bikes. They might use them on their **vacations**.

Muchas personas viajan en motos de calle. A veces las usan para salir de **vacaciones**.

One of the most important parts of a motorcycle are its **gauges**. They tell the rider how fast the bike is going.

Una de las partes más importantes de una moto es el **velocímetro**. El velocímetro marca la velocidad a la que avanza la motocicleta.

100 120 140 160 180 200 220

KM/H

RPM

13

Headlights help the biker see. They also help other people on the road see the biker.

Los faros de la motocicleta ayudan a que el piloto vea mejor. Además, ayudan a que otras personas en el camino vean la moto.

15

Some people have fun paint jobs on their bikes. These are called **custom** paint jobs.

Algunas motos tienen pintados diseños muy especiales. A éstos se les llama diseños **personalizados**.

There are people who like to buy old street bikes. Antique motorcycles can cost a lot of money.

A algunas personas les gusta comprar motos de calle viejas. Las motocicletas antiguas pueden costar mucho dinero.

19

Bikers need to wear helmets when they ride their motorcycles. This helps keep them safe.

Los pilotos de motos de calle deben usar cascos. Esto los mantiene seguros.

When you ride a motorcycle, you can feel the wind all around you. It feels like you are going faster than you really are.

Cuando montas en moto, puedes sentir el viento a tu alrededor. Esto te da la sensación de que vas más rápido de la velocidad real.

Glossary / Glosario

custom (KUS-tum) Made in a certain way for a person.

gauges (GAYJ-ez) Things that tell facts about something.

vacations (vay-KAY-shunz) Trips taken for fun.

---

personalizado(s) Hecho de manera especial para una persona.

vacaciones (las) Viajes que se hacen por diversión.

velocímetro (el) Aparato que da información sobre la velocidad de un automóvil o motocicleta.